Touchstone
From Corpus to Course Book

Michael McCarthy

CAMBRIDGE
UNIVERSITY PRESS

PUBLISHED BY THE PRESS SYNDICATE OF THE UNIVERSITY OF CAMBRIDGE
The Pitt Building, Trumpington Street, Cambridge, United Kingdom

CAMBRIDGE UNIVERSITY PRESS
The Edinburgh Building, Cambridge CB2 2RU, UK
40 West 20th Street, New York, NY 10011–4211, USA
10 Stamford Road, Oakleigh, VIC 3166, Australia
Ruiz de Alarcón 13, 28014 Madrid, Spain
Dock House, The Waterfront, Cape Town 8001, South Africa

http://www.cambridge.org

First published 2004

Printed in the United States of America

Typeface Galliard (Adobe®) 10/13 pt   *System* QuarkXPress™ 4.1   [KW]

ISBN 0 521 93481 8 paperback

Book design and typesetting by Kate Winter

Table of Contents

1 | *What is a corpus?*

A **corpus** is a collection of texts, written or spoken, usually stored in a computer database. A corpus may be quite small, for example, containing only 50,000 words of text, or very large, containing many millions of words. The Cambridge International Corpus collected by Cambridge University Press has 700 million words of text, and it is growing all the time. The plural of corpus is **corpora.**

Written texts in corpora might be drawn from books, newspapers, or magazines that have been scanned or downloaded electronically. Other written corpora might contain works of literature, or all the writings of one author (e.g., William Shakespeare). Such corpora help us to see how language is used in contemporary society, how our use of language has changed over time, and how language is used in different situations.

Spoken corpora, on the other hand, contain transcripts of spoken language. Such transcripts may be of ordinary conversations recorded in people's homes and workplaces, or of phone calls, business meetings, radio broadcasts, or TV shows. Like written corpora, spoken corpora show us how language is used in real life and in many different contexts.

People build corpora of different sizes for specific reasons. For example, a very large corpus would be required to help in the preparation of a dictionary. It might contain tens of millions of words – because it has to include many examples of all the words and expressions that are used in the language. A medium-sized corpus might contain transcripts of lectures and seminars and could be used to write books for learners who need academic language for their studies. Such corpora range in size from a million words to five or ten million words. Other corpora are more specialized and much smaller. These might contain the transcripts of business meetings, for instance, and could be used to help writers design materials for teaching business language.

The Cambridge International Corpus consists of a wide variety of both written and spoken material: from newspapers, magazines and books, to phone calls, meetings, media broadcasts, and casual conversations. The North American English part of the Corpus has helped Cambridge editors and authors to write dictionaries and other language-teaching materials.

Once a corpus is stored in a database, we can analyze it and "search" for information in the same way we use search engines to find keywords on the Internet, but with more sophisticated tools. By searching a corpus we can get answers to questions like these:

- What are the most frequent words and phrases in English?
- What are the differences between spoken and written English?

- Which tenses do people use most frequently?
- What prepositions follow particular verbs?
- How do people use words like *can, may* and *might?*
- Which words are used in more formal situations, and which are used in more informal ones?
- How often do people use idiomatic expressions and why?
- How many words must a learner know in order to participate in everyday conversation?
- How many different words do native speakers generally use in conversation?

With corpora and software tools to analyze them, we can see how language is really used. We no longer have to rely heavily on intuition to know what we say or what we write; instead we can see what hundreds of different speakers and writers have actually said or written, all at the click of a mouse.

Corpora now exist for many languages and are collected for different purposes. Learner's dictionaries, grammar reference materials, vocabulary learning materials, and, more recently, course books have all benefited from the information in corpora. Materials developed with corpora can be more authentic and can illustrate language as it is really used.

A corpus, then, is simply a large collection of texts that we can analyze using computer software, just as we can access the millions of texts on the Internet. It is not a theory of language learning or a teaching methodology, but it does influence our way of thinking about language and the kinds of texts and examples we use in language teaching.

2 | *What applications have there been in language teaching?*

Corpora have been used to design dictionaries for learners. For example, the *Cambridge Dictionary of American English* is based on a 100-million-word sample of the Cambridge International Corpus. The dictionary contains more than 40,000 words and phrases taken from the Corpus, so the learner will find all the most common language in current use. Example sentences used in the dictionary are authentic, and the definitions of words are based on how the words are actually used in the spoken and written texts of the Corpus. The dictionary writers also used the Corpus to identify the 2,000 most frequently used words that they then used to define all the other words in the dictionary. This makes the dictionary easier for learners to use. **Figure 1** shows the entry for the word *hide;* the example sentences in italics are natural and authentic because they come from the Corpus.

---

hide PREVENT FINDING /haɪd/ *v* [I/T] *past simple* **hid** /hɪd/, *past part* **hidden** /'hɪd·ᵊn/ to put (something or someone) in a place where they cannot be seen or found, or to put (yourself) somewhere where you cannot be seen or found • *She used to hide her diary under her pillow.* [T] ○ *Tommy ran and hid behind his dad.* [I] • If you hide your feelings, you do not show them: *She tried to hide her disappointment.* [T] • If you hide information from someone, you do not let that person know it: *He said nothing is wrong, but I think he's hiding something.* [T]

Figure 1: The definition of *hide* – *Cambridge Dictionary of American English,* Cambridge University Press

A major new English course called *Touchstone* is based on the North American English portion of the Cambridge International Corpus. The *Touchstone* authors have spent several years researching the Corpus, finding the most useful grammar and vocabulary for learners from a basic to an intermediate level, and finding out how people communicate in everyday situations, especially in conversation.

One way in which the *Touchstone* authors used the Corpus was to look for the most frequent and typical uses of everyday words. For example, how do people most typically use the verb *can*? As well as having the meaning "ability" (e.g., *I can swim under water*), which most teachers are familiar with, conversations in the Spoken Corpus show that an extremely common use of *can* occurs when people talk about what it is possible to do in different places and situations (e.g., *In New York, you can go to the top of the Empire State Building*). So *Touchstone* includes this meaning and gives it priority.

Another way in which the Corpus was invaluable for the authors of *Touchstone* was in answering questions that are difficult to resolve from intuition alone. For example, when do we say *he isn't working,* and when do we say *he's not working?* The Cambridge International Corpus shows that when people use nouns, they prefer the first form, *isn't,* and when they use pronouns, they prefer the second form. So *the man isn't working* is the most typical form for nouns, but *he's not working* is the most typical form for pronouns. Getting definitive answers to questions such as these means that *Touchstone* provides natural, everyday grammar which students will hear and that they can use to sound more natural themselves.

One of *Touchstone*'s many unique features is the "In conversation" boxes, where important facts about how people speak, based on the Corpus, are given. **Figure 2** shows the box for *isn't/aren't* and *'s not/'re not.*

Figure 2: The presentation of the contractions *'s not* and *'re not* – *Touchstone* Level 1, Unit 3B, Cambridge University Press

The authors of the Cambridge University Press series *Vocabulary in Use* also used the Corpus. They checked the vocabulary lists for the books against spoken and written corpora to make sure they included all the most useful vocabulary. They identified a basic vocabulary of between 1,500 and 2,000 words that are absolutely essential for everyday conversation. So *Basic Vocabulary in Use,* the lowest level of the series, teaches the 1,000 or so most important words that post-beginners (who already know about 500 words) need. What is more, the book presents the words in the same contexts and situations that are most frequent in the Corpus. So, for example, because the verb *get* is very common in descriptions of changes of state (*I'm getting tired, it's getting dark, she's getting better*), *Basic Vocabulary in Use* gives priority to this meaning.

The Corpus also shows that the basic position words *top, middle, bottom, front, side,* and *back* are all in the top 2,000 words, so *Basic Vocabulary in Use* highlights these, as shown in **Figure 3.**

the **top** of the mountain   the **middle** of the road   the **bottom** of the glass

the **front** of the car   the **side** of the car   the **back** of the car

Figure 3: The presentation of position words –
Basic Vocabulary in Use, Cambridge University Press

3 | *What kinds of information do textbook writers use from corpora?*

A corpus can be a very rich resource for writers of textbooks and other teaching materials because it gives us a detailed view of how real people speak and write in everyday situations. It can give us information about vocabulary, grammar, formality and informality, the differences between spoken and written language, how we perform such basic functions as requesting, greeting, and apologizing, how people open and close conversations, how we change the subject, how we interrupt one another, how we ask questions, and so on.

A corpus can also provide very useful statistics to help textbook writers present grammar items in the best way. Let us take as an example the verb *must*. If we look at hundreds of uses of *must* in the Spoken Corpus we find that, on average, only 5 percent of all its uses are connected with obligation (e.g., *you must have a visa to enter the United States*). Another 5 percent are in expressions such as *I must admit* and *I must say*. But the overwhelming majority of uses of *must* are in "predictive" statements such as *that must have been nice, you must be hungry*, etc. We can represent this as a graph, as shown in **Figure 4.**

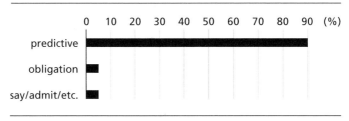

Figure 4: An analysis of the uses of *must* from the Cambridge International Corpus (Spoken Corpus)

Statistics of this kind help textbook writers set priorities in grammar teaching and find the most natural contexts for teaching grammar. We can find out what the most frequent grammar structures and grammar words are, and how they are used in speech and in writing. As mentioned before, the Corpus tells us that one of the most common uses of the verb *can* is to talk about things that are possible in different situations and places, and so the authors of *Touchstone* built conversations based on this meaning to introduce and teach *can*. **Figure 5** shows the presentation of *can* in conversation.

Textbook writers observe usage in corpora and adapt corpus texts and conversations so that they will not be intimidating or confusing for learners. In this way, teachers and learners can work with familiar types of materials, knowing that they are based on reliable and authentic sources.

Emma	Oh, no. It's raining! What can you do in New York on a rainy day? You can't take good pictures, that's for sure.
Ethan	Oh, come on. You can do a million things. We can take a ferry to the Statue of Liberty.
Emma	A ferry – in this weather?
Ethan	Well, . . . we can go to the top of the Empire State Building.
Emma	But you can't see anything in the rain.
Ethan	Yeah, you're right. I know – let's go to a Broadway show. There are shows on Wednesday afternoons.
Emma	OK. It's a deal. But first can we get an umbrella?

Figure 5: The presentation of *can* in conversation – *Touchstone* Level 1, Unit 9A, Cambridge University Press

In choosing the vocabulary to include in a course, frequency lists are very helpful for textbook writers. The *Touchstone* authors researched word lists from the Spoken and Written Corpus and made judgments about which words were the most important ones to include. For example, there is a wide range of words in English for describing colors. By searching the Corpus the authors established a list of the most common ones in order of their frequency, as seen in **Figure 6,** based on the frequency of the color words in a five-million-word sample of the Spoken North American Corpus.

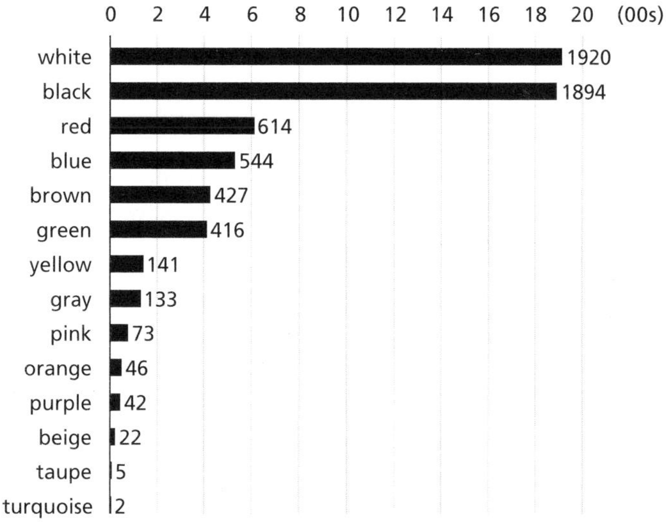

Figure 6: An analysis of the frequency of color words in North American English from the Cambridge International Corpus (Spoken Corpus)

White, black, red, blue, brown, green, yellow, gray, pink, and orange are the top 10 colors, and so we can prioritize these above the less frequent ones. *Touchstone* does this in the form of a simple "word sort" activity (**Figure 7**), and gives learners the chance to associate the color names with personal information so that they will learn them more effectively.

B What clothes and accessories do you have in these colors? Write them in the chart.
What colors do you like to wear? Discuss.

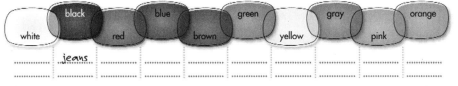

"I like to wear black. I have black jeans and a black jacket."

Figure 7: Word sort activity – *Touchstone*, Level 1, Unit 8B, Cambridge University Press

Other important types of information can be extracted from corpora apart from grammar and vocabulary. For example, when people are listening to another person, they react appropriately to what they hear. They do not simply say *yes, no,* or *uh-huh* to everything. If we search the Corpus for places where people respond, we see that people use a range of expressions that do more than merely acknowledge that they have understood. **Figure 8** shows some examples.

A: But yeah. I'm really excited about it.
B: **Oh that's great.**
A: Yeah. Thanks.

A: Yeah. He's gonna be there for the Fall semester.
B: Oh really? **Oh that's interesting.**

A: He said he learned to make very good Indian food, basically just from figuring it out from eating in Indian restaurants.
B: **That's amazing.**

Figure 8: Corpus extracts showing some common responses in conversation

Using this information, textbook writers can build speaking activities to encourage natural, appropriate responses. Here is an activity from *Touchstone*: students listen to short anecdotes and practice responding appropriately.

A 🎧 Listen to the stories. Which comment goes with which story? Number the comments.

_____ "That's terrible."　　　　　　_____ "That's so funny."
_____ "That's amazing. I bet she laughed!"　　_____ "I bet you hated it!"

B 🎧 Listen again. Think of a different comment for each story.

1. _I bet. . ._ _____　　3. _____

2. _____　　4. _____

Figure 9: An activity designed to test students' understanding of appropriate responses, from _Touchstone_ Level 2, Unit 9C, Cambridge University Press

In summary, the Corpus informs the textbook writers, who then use the information to create familiar activity types with authentic language that reflects the natural contexts of the Corpus. This helps learners to use the language more naturally in their own conversations and classroom speaking activities.

4 | *How do we analyze corpora?*

The most basic tool for analyzing the texts in a corpus is the **frequency list.** A frequency list tells us what words and phrases are used most often. **Figure 10** is a frequency list for the top 50 words in spoken North American English, based on a sample of four and a half million words of spoken data from the Cambridge International Corpus. The most frequent word – *I* – is at the top of the list.

	word	frequency		word	frequency
1	I	180,977	26	do	30,330
2	and	149,925	27	don't	29,231
3	the	145,918	28	that's	29,188
4	you	123,771	29	well	29,059
5	uh	112,031	30	for	28,687
6	to	105,596	31	what	27,038
7	a	101,731	32	on	26,360
8	that	93,381	33	think	25,020
9	it	82,708	34	right	24,383
10	of	76,347	35	not	23,123
11	yeah	67,740	36	um	22,998
12	know	65,808	37	or	22,779
13	in	57,835	38	my	22,539
14	like	48,098	39	be	22,325
15	they	45,205	40	really	20,838
16	have	43,455	41	with	20,797
17	so	42,941	42	he	20,732
18	was	41,453	43	one	20,552
19	but	40,892	44	are	20,347
20	is	40,068	45	this	20,239
21	it's	38,768	46	there	20,008
22	we	37,362	47	I'm	19,802
23	huh	36,495	48	all	19,713
24	just	32,650	49	if	19,263
25	oh	31,263	50	no	18,908

Figure 10: The top 50 words in conversation from the Cambridge International Corpus

As we can see, all the top 50 words occur thousands of times in the Corpus, so there is a huge amount of information we can learn about each word. The top 20 words occur more than 40,000 times each. Later we will see how we can simplify this amount of data so that it gives us useful information to include in teaching materials.

Here are some observations the authors of *Touchstone* made when studying this list:

- In the Spoken Corpus, *I* and *you* are some of the most frequent words of all. This is because conversation is very interactive; it's not surprising that *you* and *I* feature prominently. In the Written Corpus, however, *I* and *you* appear less frequently, because written texts are usually about "the world out there," so third-person subjects (politicians, celebrities, etc.) predominate.

- Most of the top 50 words are grammar words (pronouns, prepositions, articles, demonstratives, conjunctions, auxiliary verbs, etc.), but not all of them.

- Although *know, right, really,* and *think* are not grammar words, they occur frequently because of the expressions *you know* and *I think,* because we use *right* to agree with someone, and because of the way we use *really* to react to things people say.

- "Non-words" such as *uh, um,* and *oh* are also high-frequency items. They are important as ways of showing that one is listening and reacting. Silence is not normal in ordinary conversation, even when we're listening.

Even from this short list of 50 items we can learn a lot about how people communicate, and this information can be used to design appropriate materials and activities for the conversation class.

Frequency lists also help us to set different levels for language learning. For example, the top 1,800 or so words in the spoken frequency list are much more frequent than all the other words in the list. There is a sharp fall-off in frequency after the first 1,800, which shows us that these 1,800 words work much harder than all the others. In fact, these 1,800 words make up more than 80 percent of all the words in all the texts in the Corpus. We can therefore say that learners of English who want to be able to participate in everyday conversation must know at least these 1,800 words, or they will simply not be able to put together even a basic string of sentences. They will of course need a lot of other words to talk about themselves and the world around them, but the basic 1,800 words are the cement that holds the whole language together.

When words occur thousands of times in a corpus, it is difficult to make sense of all the uses of them, so software designers have come up with simple tools to reduce the workload. One of the most useful tools is the

concordance. A concordance is a screen display or printout of a chosen word or phrase in its different contexts, with that word or phrase arranged down the center of the display along with the text that comes before and after it. **Figure 11** shows an example of a concordance for the word *yet* in the Spoken Corpus. This is typical of what people who study corpora see on their computer screen. The user can look at screen after screen, and see *all* the different occasions in which the speakers in the Corpus have used *yet*, all together in one concordance. This screen shows a random sample of contexts for *yet*. Each line represents a different occasion of use, by a different speaker, at a different time and in a different place.

At first, the picture looks confusing. We see codes such as <1>, <2>, etc. Each speaker in every conversation is numbered one, two, three, etc. But as we look down each of these uses we see a clear pattern emerging. The overwhelming majority of uses of *yet* are in negative contexts (we have marked these here in bold), and question marks are also apparent. So the use of *yet* in negatives and in questions is an important piece of information that materials writers can take away and use in grammar materials. In this way, the materials can focus on the most central, frequent, and consequently useful aspects of a word or phrase.

We also notice that the words before *yet* are arranged alphabetically, with words beginning with "a" first *(apartment, applied, argument)*, then down through the alphabet. This concordance is "left-sorted." We can also re-sort the concordance to alphabetize the words to the right of *yet*. This would bring together all the *a*-words *(and, are)* following *yet*, then all the *b*-words *(because, been,* and *but)* and so on. Sorting is a useful tool for textbook writers as it gives us the chance to see patterns around words.

The study of **collocation** examines the likelihood that two words will occur together. So, for example, the word *blond* is likely to be used with *hair, curls, woman,* etc., but not with *car* or *jacket. Beige,* on the other hand, occurs with *carpet, jacket,* etc. but not with *hair.* So we say that *blond* **collocates** with *hair,* but *beige* does not.

With a large corpus such as the 400-million word Cambridge International Corpus, we must use computer software to analyze the data and come up with collocation statistics. The software presents us with collocation statistics in the form of simple tables that show us which words occur together most frequently. **Figure 12** is a sample of the top 20 adjectives that follow the adverb *pretty* (e.g. *it was pretty good*), and how often they occur in a five million-word sample of the spoken North American Corpus.

Imagine if you had to count those 939 examples of *pretty good* by hand! The software does it in a split second. With this knowledge, we can present the most frequent and useful contexts for *pretty,* or any other words or phrases in the Corpus. Therefore, learning words with their most frequent collocates is a good learning habit that can start right from the lowest levels.

```
 1  that.  <2> I don't have an apartment          yet  but I will starting in October.
 2  Washington that's why I haven't applied       yet  because of the competition.
 3  If you haven't fleshed out the argument       yet  you know then that's what we'
 4  in the morning and I wasn't even awake        yet  and uh someone who was staying over
 5  <2> Hmm. Did you play the Carmen CD           yet  mom at all or..?  <3> No.  <2> N
 6  you just I don't know. Not comfortable        yet  but then I became very comfortable t
 7  And uh prices don't seem much different       yet  but you just wait 'til January and w
 8  s well.  <1> Did you have your dinner         yet  Thelma or not?  <5> No. Not yet.
 9  re.  <1> We're not ready to do dinner         yet  are we?  <2> No.  <1> Do you wan
10  ade it. I didn't look at the directions       yet  but...  <1> Oh okay.  <4> It loo
11  ke every you know.  <1> He didn't eat         yet  did he?  <2> No I'm holding him.
12  gets gets bigger but it doesn't explode       yet  because all that energy hasn't been
13  hat one doesn't get the get the flowers       yet  either.  <1> No.  <2> Maybe it's
14  hem in a dark room. And it didn't grow.        Yet  my bagels on the counter molded wit
15  ix of the teachers because there hasn't       yet  been one and...  <2> Is there a li
16  even know but we're here now and I have        yet  to eat anything.  <5> Or whatever
17  me constraint. We don't know what it is       yet  cause we don't know how long it's go
18  out yet and they don't know what it is        yet  cause it could mean that something's
19  omen's size eight. I'm not done with it       yet  though. I've got to do the other one
20  gned it yet.  <2> He hasn't signed it         yet  and I'd like to add that clause abou
21  now if... I don't think she'll start it       yet. I don't know. She may. If she says
22  happen. You don't... I haven't seen it        yet  but it doesn't mean I never will. If
23  m not ready to give up on the idea just       yet  because it seems like there's someth
24  mini write up for those who don't know        yet  is like two paragraphs. Let's say yo
25  b things to these two but we don't know        yet  right?  <2> Yeah. Well we... He di
26  s before the prom still hasn't asked me       yet  and I'm sitting there like what and
27  our parents met or why haven't they met       yet  and they said well I don't know we t
28  <3> The only one that you have not met        yet  met would be uh Tommy. His son. You have
```

Figure 11: A concordance of *yet* from the Cambridge International Corpus

	pretty +	frequency		pretty +	frequency
1	good	939	11	easy	41
2	nice	96	12	high	37
3	bad	87	13	busy	28
4	cool	80	14	tough	28
5	big	72	15	small	28
6	close	58	16	expensive	27
7	neat	58	17	scary	27
8	sure	52	18	hard	24
9	interesting	46	19	far	22
10	funny	43	20	lucky	21

Figure 12: The top 20 adjectives that follow the adverb *pretty,* from the Cambridge International Corpus

These tools and the frequency lists, concordances, and collocation statistics they generate enable textbook writers to get at the facts about language use in a way that would be very difficult to do by using intuition alone, or by studying a small number of texts. The computer software makes it possible to examine thousands of texts in the Corpus at the same time; in this way, we get a bird's eye view of the language as it has been used by a very large number of speakers and writers. In the case of *Touchstone,* this means that the content we present is authentic and based on accurate information about present-day usage.

5 How are corpus-informed materials different?

The advantages of using corpora in the development of language instruction materials are undoubtedly great, but we have not lost sight of the need to balance the use of corpus data with the need for a carefully crafted syllabus that takes into account sound teaching methodology and practical classroom requirements. Achieving that balance requires more traditional skills – those of writers and editors – as well as the benefits of classroom experience.

The authors of *Touchstone* have consequently spent long hours interpreting and mediating their corpus research with three broad goals in mind:

- To identify authentic, motivating language
- To weave their findings into a carefully crafted syllabus
- To create course books that are familiar in structure and easy to use

As we have discussed, it is important that teachers and learners encounter authentic language in motivating contexts. In this sense, "mediating" data means finding the clearest and best examples to use from the Corpus. These examples are chosen to suit the interests of learners and to be most relevant to their lives. The authors construct dialogs and activities that present items in a natural way – that is, in a way that reflects the character and content of the conversations in the Corpus.

It is important to note that corpus data alone does not dictate an instructional syllabus. Rather, such data are considered in light of other pedagogical requirements and used to inform the *Touchstone* syllabus in significant ways. For instance, the introduction of high-frequency language does not take priority over issues such as the introduction of basic, functional (though not necessarily high-frequency) language for beginning learners. Similarly, presenting vocabulary in logical or thematic groups remains a sound organizing principle that we use in *Touchstone*, despite the inevitable need to include some (relatively) low-frequency words in vocabulary lists.

Teachers and learners should expect that, in most ways, corpus-informed materials will look like traditionally prepared materials. The presentation of new language and activity types will be familiar. Certainly, teachers do not need any additional knowledge to use them.

Beneath the surface, however, corpus-informed materials are genuinely special in the following ways:

- They are based on actual usage.
- The examples used in them, although they may sometimes be edited or adapted, are a reflection of real usage; they are not invented.

- The syllabus (the items to be taught as well as the sequence in which they will be presented) is informed by frequency information: For instance, we can prioritize grammar and vocabulary that is most frequent and most useful.

- The contexts in which words and grammar structures are used are authentic ones, based on the contexts that occur in corpora.

- The presentation and activities can focus on the important differences between spoken and written language.

- The materials can include language that was ignored or not noticed in the past but that is at the heart of real communication. For example, when we report other people's words, we often say *Mary said* or *Daniel told me,* but the corpus shows we also frequently say *Mary was saying* or *Daniel was telling me,* especially when we have some interesting news to pass on. The *was + -ing* construction for reporting speech has gone unnoticed in the past, even in comprehensive grammar reference books.

- Specialized corpora can be analyzed to meet the needs of particular groups of learners. For example, we can use an academic corpus collected in university and college contexts to help learners who are going to study abroad, or a business corpus to construct materials for businesspeople who need to work in a second language.

- The writers of corpus-informed materials can anticipate common errors by looking at corpora of learners' work from a wide variety of language backgrounds.

- Students don't have to live in the target language environment to experience authentic language – it's right there, in their course books and dictionaries.

So, although they may not look very different from traditional texts, corpus-informed materials are revolutionary in the way they bring real usage into the classroom.

6 | *How do corpus-informed textbooks help teachers and learners more than traditional ones?*

Successful learning is all about motivation. Corpus-informed materials motivate because teachers and learners can be sure that the language they are practicing is modern, used in everyday situations, targeted to situations they are likely to find themselves in, and corresponds to what they will hear and see in real conversations, movies, radio and TV shows, newspapers, books, Internet texts, and magazines. It is not artificial or invented language, but consists of the most widely used words, phrases, and grammar.

Because we can be more certain about what language is essential to basic communication and what language allows us to speak more precisely and with greater sophistication, corpus-informed materials can take learners to their goals quicker and more efficiently.

By using spoken corpora we can also learn very important things about social communication. As a result, the activities in corpus-informed materials can focus on the most important features of speaking and listening skills and produce more effective communication.

7 | *What will we see in the future?*

In the future we can expect bigger corpora, perhaps consisting of billions of words, and software that will be able to transcribe conversations automatically. We can expect more sophisticated tools to do the kinds of searching that at present cannot be done automatically, for example, finding idioms. At least for now, a computer does not know what an idiom is!

We can also expect more and better corpus-informed materials, perhaps in electronic format, on DVD, or accessible on the Internet. Perhaps these materials will include hyperlinks to actual corpora or to corpus samples so that teachers and students can explore and investigate language for themselves. And we can expect more user-friendly home- and classroom-based facilities in which teachers and learners can build and explore their own corpora. Our corpora will become more sophisticated and ever more finely tuned to our needs. The future is exciting, and corpora are here to stay.

8 | *Appendices*

Glossary

Here are some basic terms you will hear when people talk about corpora.

collocate (noun)   a word that has a tendency to occur next to or near another word: *hair* and *curls* are collocates of *blond*

collocate (verb)   to have a tendency to occur together: *blond* collocates with *hair*; *blond* does not collocate with *carpet*

collocation   a meaningful co-occurrence of two words next to or near each other

concordance   a screen display or printout showing a key word or phrase in many different contexts of use, in which the key word or phrase is usually arranged in a vertical column in the center of the display along with the text that comes before and after it

corpus (plural **corpora**)   a large collection of texts, usually stored on a computer

frequency list   an arrangement of words, non-words *(uh, huh)*, phrases or grammatical items in order of how often they occur in a corpus, usually starting with the most frequent

Table of figures

Figure 9: An activity designed to test students' understanding of appropriate responses, from *Touchstone* Level 2, Unit 9C, Cambridge University Press

Figure 10: The top 50 words in conversation from the Cambridge International Corpus

Figure 11: A concordance of *yet* from the Cambridge International Corpus

Figure 12: The 20 top adjectives that follow the adverb *pretty*, from the Cambridge International Corpus

Further reading

The following books and articles are recommended if you want to learn more about corpora.

Biber, Douglas, Susan Conrad, and Randi Reppen. (1998). *Corpus Linguistics. Investigating language structure and use.* Cambridge: Cambridge University Press.

Hunston, Susan. (2002). *Corpora in Applied Linguistics.* Cambridge: Cambridge University Press.

O'Keeffe, Anne, & Fiona Farr. (2003). "Using language corpora in initial teacher education: pedagogic issues and practical applications." *TESOL Quarterly* 37 (3): 389-418. This article contains a useful list of Web sites connected to the study of corpora.

Rundell, Michael, and Penny Stock. (1992). "The corpus revolution." Three-part article in *English Today* 8/2, 8/3, 8/4.

Sinclair, John. (1991). *Corpus, Concordance, Collocation.* Oxford: Oxford University Press.

If you want to find out more about corpora and software, visit Michael Barlow's Web page at Rice University, Texas: http://www.ruf.rice.edu/~barlow/corpus.html

Find out about the American National Corpus, a major corpus of spoken and written North American English, at http://americannationalcorpus.org